Dividing Lines

Líneas Divisorias

Dividing Lines
Líneas Divisorias

Beatriz Pizano

Playwrights Canada Press
Toronto

Top front jacket photo © Jeremy Mimnagh
Interior photos on pages 2, 6, 10, 25, 31, 41, 44, 58, 62, 66, 73, 83, 102, and 111
© Jeremy Mimnagh
Interior photos on pages 35, 49, 52, 78, 87, 95, 98, and 106 © Trevor Schwellnus

Playwrights Canada Press
202-269 Richmond St. W. Toronto, ON M5V 1X1
416.703.0013 | info@playwrightscanada.com | www.playwrightscanada.com

LIBRARY AND ARCHIVES CANADA CATALOGUING IN PUBLICATION
Title: Dividing lines = Líneas Divisorias / Beatriz Pizano.
Names: Pizano, Beatriz, author.
Description: A play.
Identifiers: Canadiana (print) 20220279829 | Canadiana (ebook) 2022027987X
  | ISBN 9780369103796 (softcover) | ISBN 9780369103819 (PDF)
  | ISBN 9780369103802 (HTML)
Classification: LCC PS8631.I93 D58 2022 | DDC C812/.6—dc23

Playwrights Canada Press operates on land which is the ancestral home of the Anishinaabe Nations (Ojibwe / Chippewa, Odawa, Potawatomi, Algonquin, Saulteaux, Nipissing, and Mississauga), the Wendat, and the members of the Haudenosaunee Confederacy (Mohawk, Oneida, Onondaga, Cayuga, Seneca, and Tuscarora), as well as Metis and Inuit peoples. It always was and always will be Indigenous land.

We acknowledge the financial support of the Canada Council for the Arts, the Ontario Arts Council (OAC), Ontario Creates, and the Government of Canada for our publishing activities.

To Trevor Schwellnus, who held my mother's hand and mine on stage and off. Marce, mi ángel. Vicky and Caliche, my heart. Y Julia, por siempre y para siempre.

Playwright's Notes

This is a journey of love—its possibilities . . . and impossibilities. The story is based on truths, many of them personal, remembered over time. My desire with this sharing is to look at death with respect, compassion, and without fear. To honour life . . . and our choices. We don't exist in isolation. We are watersheds connected by histories and experiences.

How do you make a decision about dying for someone who can no longer make it for themselves? For someone you love? These decisions are extremely hard to make, and extremely personal. I am not advocating for anyone to choose this path. I'm only offering possibilities, without judgment, without formulas.

For myself, I do not believe in unnecessary suffering. Love is truly being able to let go.

This play addresses an underserved conversation: we need to speak about death, about how we want to die, about how we can prepare as a society for this difficult step.

The story is personal.

I spent a decade witnessing my mother's unbearable suffering. Added to that was my own immigrant story. I was Julia's only daughter and I was living thousands of miles away from her. I was not able to bring her here to live with me. How I arrived at a very difficult decision was in part based on my journey as an immigrant, as a woman from the Americas. I sought inspiration in ritual, in other traditions that don't shy away from the conversation. I wanted to include historical context to the piece because I believe our choices are informed by our collective histories and our personal experiences.

—Beatriz Pizano
September 2022

Director's Notes

This script was developed as a presentation in a small amphitheatre. Downstage centre is a small intimate space: a table with a number of photos on it, hidden shelves for props, and a camera overhead to capture what Beatriz is doing with the photos. This setup functions as an overhead projection / live PowerPoint arrangement. The physical photos—little embodiments of her private past—are important.

The stage is otherwise open, with a back wall and floor covered in the same soft texture. Upstage right and left are boxes for Beatriz to sit on. The entire area—floor, boxes, and back wall— is a video projection surface to show the audience what Beatriz is looking at on her private table.

When she steps away from her table Beatriz enters a public space. As she moves up stage, she merges into the field of video projection, and the video becomes a pastiche of public histories that enfold her. In these moments the feeling of the amphitheatre—a public forum where citizens discuss matters that affect us all—is more strongly felt.

Downstage: private history and personal connection. Centre / up stage: public history and the global, political, cultural context around her.

We note some actions through stage directions, to clarify the moment at hand. Most of these are visual descriptions of images or of text in translation that support Beatriz when she speaks Spanish. As much as possible, these are on pieces of paper, and not special effects.

Beatriz's voice—speaking proper names in the manner she would in Colombia—is maintained, indicated at times by Spanish accents and spellings.

The music in this show was originally created with the composer playing live with the actor.

Because this show was created both at the writing table and in the rehearsal room, this script is ultimately the last version of the play as it was performed. As such, it might be read as a document of a cultural moment, as a personal history, as a public consideration of the intersection of several social issues (assisted dying, the many challenges of migration, translation across languages and cultures, the personal and political emancipation of women, and more), or, finally, as a formula for bringing this experiment back to life.

For us, it was a conversation. May it continue.

—Trevor Schwellnus
September 2022

Dividing Lines | Líneas Divisorias was first produced by Aluna Theatre at the Theatre Centre, Toronto, from November 18 to December 2, 2018, with the following cast and crew:

Beatriz Pizano: Writer / Performer
Trevor Schwellnus: Director / Dramaturg / Scenographer
Brandon Valdivia: Original Composition / Sound Designer
Andjelija Djuric: Costume Designer
Sandy Plunkett: Stage Manager
Rebecca Vandevelde: Production Manager / Associate Lighting Designer
Pip Bradford: Associate Production Manager
Bruce Gibbons Fell: Development Support
Victoria Mata Soledad: Movement Coach
Sue Balint: Producer
Photographer: Jeremy Mimnagh

In August 2022, the play was selected to be presented in New York as part of the Completed Life Initiative, an end-of-life non-profit focusing on expanding death with dignity legislation.

Since the 2018 production, the state of legislation around assisted dying in Canada (and Colombia) has been changing. Thank you to Dying with Dignity Canada for maintaining up-to-date information on the state of the changing legal landscape on these issues in Canada: www.dyingwithdignity.ca.

PROLOGUE
the invitation

We hear a heartbeat and breathing—in and out.

Imagine:

You are a raindrop.

We hear a single raindrop, which continues to echo.

The top of a mountain in the Andes.

We hear the sound of the wind. A video of an abstract, dynamic sky is projected on the walls, with a map of the Americas projected on the floor.

If you fall to the west side of the watershed line, you will flow down into the Pacific Ocean, but if you drop to the east, even by one foot, you flow down to the Amazon basin and into the Atlantic Ocean, and end up on the other side of the world.

In Spanish the word watershed is translated simply as the dividing line of the waters, La línea divisoria de las aguas. But in English it also means a momentous dividing point that changes the direction of a life . . . an exact moment in time after which we will never be the same—and yet we only recognize that watershed moment in hindsight.

Wherever we stand, we're standing in a watershed.

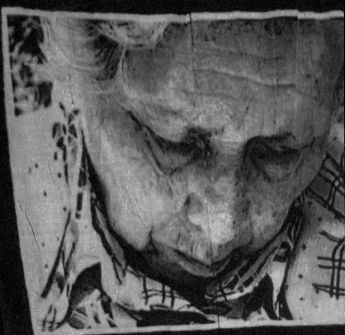

EPISODE I

This is not a drama.

This is a conversation about dying. The only thing we all have in common in this room. We may differ on how we want to get there.

Beatriz places a photo of Julia with her eyes closed in the nursing home.

Julia, my mother, lives the last years of her life in a nursing home. She struggles with Alzheimer's. I call it El Calvario de Julia. Julia's calvary. Any Catholics in the house?

The calvary is the site where Jesus is crucified. On the way to his death, he walks La Via Dolorosa, the Path of Suffering. He experiences agonizing physical and mental pain.

In Colombia we use the word calvario for any challenging emotional situation. We like to exaggerate. It's a cultural thing. "Ay mija, eso es un calvario."

In my mother's case, the metaphor fits. At the end of her life Julia cannot walk, talk, or make decisions anymore.

How do we make a decision about dying—for someone we love?

EPISODE 2
*the first memory changes the
direction of a life*

My family history is a fiction. A fable with animals and strange happenings and a moral lesson at the end.

Beatriz places a photo of herself: she is two years old and holds an old phone that is almost as big as she is.

This is the first photograph that exists of me. No baby pictures. My first memory.

We don't form conscious memories until the ages of three or four—because we don't have the language to report on those memories. (*referring to the photograph*) At two years old my vocabulary doesn't exceed more than fifty words. Like a newcomer, in their first year of arriving in Toronto, or when you go on holidays to a resort in Mexico or Cuba.

I may not remember the event . . . but I remember the feelings around the event, and those will have the greatest impact on my life.

The memory begins. Lights and video shift, the sound reverberates—large indistinct figures loom.

I'm laughing.

Running naked down a corridor.

Women chase after me.

A closed door. Inside . . . I stop laughing. A white room. IV tubes. A woman lies on a white bed. Men dressed in white chase me out of the room.

The memory ends.

For a long time, I thought this memory was a fantasy I had created. But *(places a photo of Amparo)* my birth mother, Amparo, dies in our home at the age of twenty-seven. She leaves behind three little children— *(places a drawing)* Vicky, six years old, Caliche is five, and I'm two. I don't have a photograph, so our lovely and talented director made this. Thank you, Trevor.

Beatriz points at the characters in the drawing.

Our father—

Beatriz places the photo of Fabio. The drawing is between the photos of Amparo and Fabio.

I call him the Marlboro Man because he modelled as a cowboy in a cigarette ad back in the day when smoking was fashionable— The Marlboro Man rides away into the distance after his beloved wife passes.

Beatriz removes the photos of Amparo and Fabio and replaces them with photos of Julia and Jorge, placing them on top of the drawing so they block out the two other children.

But his sister, Julia, my aunt *(points to photo)*, and her husband Jorge, my uncle, in some twist of fate, will become my parents. But not yet.

Beatriz places a photo of Julia on her honeymoon—she is by the water.

This is Julia on her honeymoon. At this moment in time she has no idea that one day she will become my adoptive mother. She's still dreaming of the many children she will have.

Julia loves water, the stars, and the immensity of the universe.

I . . . I'm terrified of that immensity.

Unlike me, Julia would rather live outside this world.

I only want to be in a world I can see and touch. Like that guy in the Bible . . . the one who has to put his finger in the wound to believe . . .

(to audience) What's his name?

> *If they need encouragement, she chides them—"Come on, Catholics!" Someone yells out the name.*

Thomas! Doubting Thomas. That's me!

(to audience) Thank you!

> *Beatriz places a photo of Jorge and Beatriz sitting outside.*

Jorge is a romantic and a walking contradiction.

This is the first picture that exists of the two of us. I'm around four or five years old . . . I remember this moment so clearly. Jorge comes home one day with the latest invention. A camera that takes photos on its own!

> *Beatriz makes the same pose as she does in the photograph and counts down:*

Three, two, one!

> *We hear the camera: ka-chick!*

Jorge gives me three important life lessons:

Beatriz changes the photo to one of her at ten years old.

Lesson number one: Asegúrate de estudiar una carrera para que nunca, nunca te tengas que quedar con alguien a quien no amas.

At ten years old he wants me to promise him that I will have a career, so I NEVER, NEVER have to stay with someone I don't love. I never have.

Lesson number two:

Beatriz places a picture of herself at her fifteenth birthday.

I'm fifteen years old. A big deal. A rite of passage when a girl officially becomes a woman. She is introduced into society.

Since my first period I have become a fierce atheist—who is forced to take religion classes in school. In Colombia the state and the church have a marriage of sorts.

My revenge . . . I refuse to read the Bible. My religious studies come mainly from movies—the ones of Roman men in skirts and sandals in the Colosseum. Oh, and *Jesus Christ Superstar* . . . oh, my God, I love that movie. Don't you?

Beatriz possibly interacts with the audience.

Oh, come on, raise your hands . . . we're in a theatre. My lips are sealed.

I confess! I have the entire soundtrack on my iPhone!

It's the remnants of the Catholic girl. It's in my DNA.

According to our director, Trevor, I have "the conscience of a Catholic, but not the culture." Meaning: I have the guilt—mea culpa, mea culpa, mea maxima culpa—the punishment—

Beatriz motions as if hitting herself with a whip.

Culpa, culpa, culpa, hijue puta—but I don't know anything about the Testament. What is there to know? There's the before, and after.

And now that I am fifteen and officially a woman, I demand to be taken out of religion classes.

Julia . . . Julia, all of a sudden, decides to become a believer.

JULIA: Que conste que yo si soy una creyente.

I have never seen my mother go to church . . . except for weddings and funerals.

Jorge is more than happy to abide. My father hates religion. He hates the church. Even though all his aunts are missionary nuns stationed in conflict-ridden countries across the Americas.

A change in location.

Principal's office. The Columbus School. A bilingual high school for the all the petit bourgeois just like me.

Jorge emerges with a sombre face.

JORGE: ¡Este es un país de mierda! Nada que hacer.

Nothing to be done.

And he gives me his second lesson.

JORGE: Un día tu decidirás . . . ley o no ley.

"One day I will decide, no matter what the law says."

Beatriz places the photo of Julia at the end of her life on top of Jorge's lesson.

At this moment in time, I have no idea Julia will end up alone, living in a nursing home. I have no idea that I will hold my mother's future in my hands.

Lesson number three:

Beatriz places a photograph of her graduation.

I'm eighteen years old. I have graduated from high school and I still have no idea what "career" I want to study. My classmates have all chosen a path—they will become doctors, businessmen, mothers . . . just like their parents.

I have two choices: to become a revolutionary or a petit bourgeois . . . I can't make up my mind!

Shift—a historical reel plays with a video map on the floor and news images on the wall behind Beatriz.

In my short life there have been military coups in:

Argentina, Bolivia, Brasil . . . Chile . . . República Dominicana . . . Ecuador, El Salvador, Guatemala, Honduras, Panamá, Perú! y Uruguay . . . and many contra and requecontra revolutions. Isabel Perón becomes the first woman president in the world. Will women finally bring change? . . . Well, she turns out to be a fucking disaster. Don't worry, sisters, one woman doesn't represent us all!

After much thinking, and serious consideration, I choose to become a Bohemian. Jorge agrees—

Beatriz is surprised.

—gives me a one-year free pass and his third and last lesson:

Personal freedom . . . termina en el momento en el que otra persona se involucra.

Beatriz translates.

" . . . Personal freedom ends at the moment when your actions affect someone else's life."

Beatriz removes the photograph of her graduation and Jorge's lesson and replaces them with a picture of her about to get married.

By the end of the Bohemian year, I have chosen a career . . . a husband . . . and I'm moving to Canada . . .

Shift—a historical reel plays with a video map on the floor and news images/videos on the walls behind Beatriz.

Times are changing. Joe Clark becomes the youngest prime minister in Canada, defeating Trudeau the first and ending sixteen years of continuous Liberal rule.

Pink Floyd releases *The Wall*.

Beatriz sings, adapting the lyrics of "Another Brick in the Wall":

We don't need no landed status . . .

I have no idea that from this moment on Spanish will become the language of my past.

(sings) We don't need no border patrol . . .

And that from now on I will live a life in translation.

(*sings*) *Detention centres for our peoples . . .*

A future . . . in a language that has no connections to my roots, to my ancestors, to my mothers, to my history, to my land.

(*sings*) HEY—MIGRA, LEAVE THOSE KIDS ALONE!

Well, Jorge is thrilled that I'm moving to Canada— WITH THE BOYFRIEND—and becoming an immigrant, his dream—

But being the non-Catholic Catholic girl—woman—that I am . . .

> *Beatriz places a photo of herself in her wedding dress.*

(*an aside*) By the way, I designed the dress—

> **BEA:** (*as if speaking to her father*) I have a confession to make: nos vamos a casar—
>
> (*as if Jorge hadn't understood*) Marry—

> *Jorge is waiting for what comes next.*

> Marry in the church!

> **JORGE:** (*pulling his hair and walking around*) ¿Por la iglesia? ¿Por la puta iglesia?

Jorge pleads. He never pleads.

> **JORGE:** ¡Váyanse a vivir juntos! Live together!

> **BEA:** Living together?! Out of the question!

Not because of me. But my soon-to-be husband comes from an aristocratic, conservative, and super Catholic family, the worst possible combination ever.

> **BEA:** (*throwing the lesson back at Jorge*) Personal freedom, Jorge! Your words, not mine!

I win. I always win with my father.

All the preparations for the wedding are underway. Until a tiny word embedded in my birth certificate changes the direction of everything.

> *Beatriz places her birth certificate.*

> *She points at the word.*

A/DOP/TA/DA.   A/DOP/TED.

Jorge goes ballistic. Somehow this four-syllable word in Spanish and three syllables in English . . . it always takes so many more words to say anything in Spanish . . . this word threatens my father's identity as a father. This man who has defied his own asphyxiating classist society and its rules is suddenly crumbling in the presence of a tiny word.

> **JORGE:** ¡Hay que borrar esa palabra!

He wants us to erase the word . . . Or there will be no wedding. And there is no way I can win this one.

But how do we change a legal document?

Julia comes to the rescue. We the women devise a master plan.

This is the moment when I learn two important teachings from Julia.

Teaching number one: the power of women. Together we change the laws dictated by men.

A video of the curia of Medellín plays. We hear church music—Gregorian chants. Beatriz makes the sign of the cross.

La curia de Medellín. From the Latin *coviria,* "a gathering of men" . . . the only earthly power that can erase my lineage.

The church music continues—a corridor of light.

A door . . . inside. The archbishop of Medellín sits behind a gigantic desk. In el nombri del padri, del hijo y del espiritu santi—*(whispering)* something like that. This is the only man who has the power to legitimize me?

After what feels like an eternity we are allowed to state our case.

Beatriz sings from Jesus Christ Super Star, *becoming more defiant as she goes:*

I don't know how to love him . . .

We beg.

What to do

We implore.

How to move him.

We pray.

He's a man—

We fast—okay, I exaggerate.

He's just a man . . . and I've had so many
Men before, in very many ways . . . yes

My mother stops me before I lose it.

She brings out the deadly weapon—

Video: a slow reveal of a giant dessert.

> **JULIA:** Su excelencia, a temptation no holy man can resist—
> *(offering the dessert to the archbishop)* Dessert?

Julia's teaching number two: never underestimate sweetness.

> *Beatriz triumphantly pulls the new birth certificate out of her*
> *bosom, or somewhere else.*

With a new given identity in hand, into the church we go.

> *Lights: a church aisle.*

Music, maestro.

> *Organ music is played.*

I actually didn't allow any organ music to be played in the church
but I need it to set the scene.

> *Beatriz moves as if walking down the aisle.*

Oh, my God! What the F am I doing? Do I really, really love this
man? Do I really want to move to another country and leave
everything behind—

> **VOICE OF PRIEST:** Hasta que la muerte los separe . . .

"Until death do us part?!" Oh, my God. God, please, please, allow me to last one year? Like Joe Clark?

Which I do, to the day.

Beatriz places another photo.

This is me in Vancouver. I want a divorce.

His family wants an annulment.

An annulment declares that a marriage has never actually taken place.

She points at the picture in the church.

But they need me to declare myself an adulteress.

And somehow this four-syllable word—both in English and Spanish—awakens the rebel in me. The free woman my father has been fighting so hard for me to become. The young woman who has been raised on revolutionary songs and Rod Stewart . . . yes, I love him! I'm a romantic . . .

No, this WOMAN will NOT take the blame! My history will not be erased by the Catholic church ever again.

EPISODE 3

my life began as a revolution

I was conceived in an era of revolution.

Shift—a historical reel plays with a video map on the floor and news images/videos on the wall behind Beatriz.

Camilo Torres, the Revolutionary Priest in Colombia declares, "If Jesus were alive today, he would be a guerrillero."

Fidel Castro addresses the United Nations as the newly elected prime minister of La República de Cuba.

(*quoting Fidel*) "The National General Assembly of the Cuban People condemns the exploitation of man by man, and the exploitations of under-developed countries by imperialists capital."

The population of Latin America is two hundred million.

The FDA in the United States of America approves the birth control pill, granting greater reproductive rights to women.

The Canadian Bill of Rights passes.

The Diefenbaker government decides to "permit" all Status Indians to vote in federal elections.

The Quiet Revolution declares . . . "Masters in our own house— maîtres chez nous." Revolutions are never quiet.

Ontario euthanizes ten thousand cats due to overpopulation. I love cats!

The National Theatre School opens in Montreal. I will not attend that school.

She takes a breath.

I could have been born anywhere, in any particular time and place, but I arrive in the land that lost its name after the three ships arrived: *La Pinta, La Niña, y La Santa María*. Abya Yala, Turtle Island, a land of vital blood, a land in its full maturity.

A land of genocide. A land where in less than two hundred years, 120 million Indigenous people are erased. And we don't even know their names. A land we now call Las Américas. PLURAL, mi amor. Let us not be confused. We are a continent.

Las Américas, a land where languages are erased. Millions are displaced, disappeared, and enslaved. Las Américas, a land where hundreds of women are murdered and nobody cares. Las Américas, a land where lands are stolen, walls are built, borders are patrolled so the rich get richer and the poor get poorer and we wonder why wars never end.

I was born en la tierra del olvido, the land of forgetfulness . . . into a family where no one remembers.

The music stops.

Years ago, when the Marlboro Man was sick in a hospital in Colombia, I'm doing my astrological chart, and I need him to tell me . . . in case he . . . you know . . .

She does not want to say "dies."

BEA: What time of the day was I born?

MARLBORO MAN: ¡Ah, yo no me acuerdo!

BEA: Of course he doesn't remember—he wasn't at my birth. You'll see.

MARLBORO MAN: Pero todos en Medellín nacen como al medio día.

BEA: Everyone in Medellín is born around noon . . .

And that is that.

But this is the official story of me.

From the moment my birth mother Amparo experiences a contraction, there's little time for anything else but to give birth.

Vicky, my sister, is the only one who makes it to the delivery room.

Caliche, my brother, is delivered in the car . . . on the way to the hospital.

And me . . .well . . .

The Marlboro Man is nowhere to be seen. He's with his horses.

So my uncle Jorge and my aunt Julia drive my mother to the hospital. And I am born in the elevator—

Going down.

The doctor dressed in white hands me to Jorge:

DOCTOR: "Felicitaciones, tiene una hija."

JORGE: Yo no soy el papá . . .

BEA: (to audience) What?!He's not my father?

We hear the cries of a newborn.

JORGE: *(offers the crying baby to Julia)* Julia . . . ?

Julia doesn't take me.

Beat.

Maybe I remind her of her stillborn baby.

Although at this very moment no one knows it yet, I will become Julia and Jorge's only child.

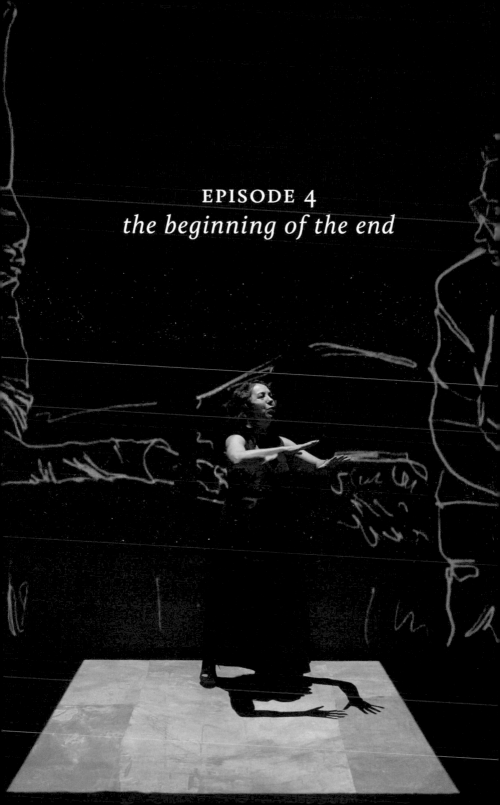

EPISODE 4
the beginning of the end

Year one of Julia's calvary.

Shift—a historical reel plays with news images/videos on the wall behind Beatriz.

In this year, a major blackout hits Canada and the US.

In this year, the United States launches war on Iraq.

And in this year, the Human Genome Project maps the DNA of the human body, giving us a better understanding of the role of genetics in human health and disease.

I fly to Medellín.

I put Julia in a nursing home.

A video is projected of herself and Julia in the nursing home.

The first night she can't find her way back to her room.

She claims she sleeps under a tree, by the water fountain, next to the bird sanctuary.

Did it happen?

Or did she imagine it?

Julia walks into the empty dining room.

Desserts are placed on the tables.

With her spoon Julia samples each and every dessert.

By the end of year one, Julia eats a bar of soap. Foam comes out of her mouth.

   Beat.

Julia is beginning to disappear.

EPISODE 5
death and guilt

Shift—a historical reel plays with news images/videos on the wall behind Beatriz.

I'm two years old.

In this year, John Glenn becomes the first American to orbit the Earth . . .

In this year, we come to the brink of a nuclear war—the Cuban Missile Crisis—

In this year, García Márquez publishes "Big Mama's Funeral." "Los funerales de la Mamá Grande." And this year our mamá grande disappears.

What follows is a reconstruction, in condensed form, of what takes place after Amparo dies and the Marlboro Man rides away into the distance . . .

> *Beatriz places the drawing of herself and her siblings.*

Caliche draws and sings his private lullaby.

> *We hear the voice of Caliche as an adult singing. Beatriz sings and dances. Slowly her microphone is affected to sound like a child throughout the scene.*

Cachito, Cachito, Cachito mío
Pedazo de cielo que Dios me dió
Te miro y te miro y al fin bendigo
Bendigo la suerte de ser tu amor

Julia and an army of aunties have come to take us back to Medellín to live with our old, old, old grandparents.

Beatriz places a drawing of Amparo in Heaven.

They tell us that our mother, who is in the sky with the angels, will come back . . . one of these days.

(*disbelief*) I have never seen an angel myself.

I see: sadness.

I hear: whispers . . .

I smell the fear in the adults.

Caliche and I stand our ground. We are going nowhere until our mommy comes back. We have to let her know what's happening. But how?

Caliche knows how to draw!

Beatriz places a drawing of a little parrot.

We will attach a message to his little parrot's paw and send it to the sky where only birds can go—I think it's the best idea ever.

Vicky walks in, grabs the parrot before it can take off, bites off its head, and spits it on the ground.

She places a drawing of Vicky biting off the head of the parrot.

VICKY: Las mamás se mueren porque los niños son malos. ¡Malos!

"Mothers die because their children are bad."

Two new words are added to my vocabulary: Death. Guilt.

Beatriz places a drawing of an airplane.

As we fly with the aunties back to Medellín in the giant silver bird through the sky, I confirm: there are no people living in the sky. Death is irreversible, definite, and permanent.

EPISODE 6
Julia forgets me

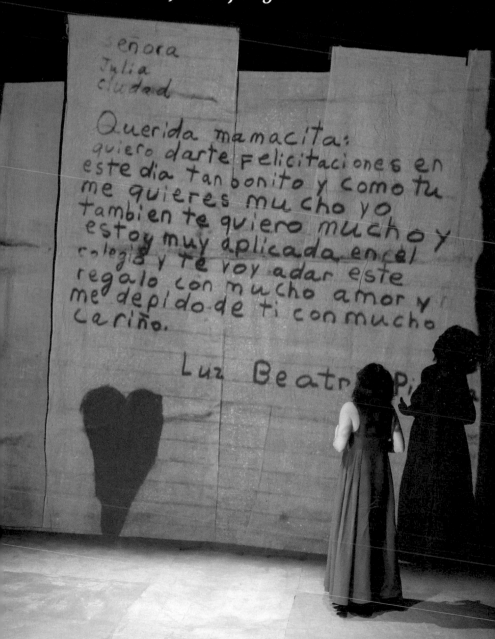

Shift.

Year two of Julia's calvary.

Mother's Day.

I'm in Canada.

Julia is in the nursing home. I call her.

> **JULIA:** (*voice over*) ¿Y usted quién es?

> **BEA:** (*in shock*) Who am I?!

Alzheimer's is irreversible, definite, and permanent.

> *Beat.*

> *Beatriz places a Mother's Day card. She translates it for the audience.*

This is a Mother´s Day card that I wrote for Julia when I was eight years old: "Dear Mamacita"—mamacita is also a word you use to flirt with, I think it still is—"I want to congratulate you on this beautiful day and since you love me so much I also love you very much and I'm doing very well in school and I'm going to give you this little present with a lot of love and I say farewell with fondness."

> *Beat.*

I have been erased.

> *Beat.*

If we are not remembered . . . who are we?

EPISODE 7
inviting the audience to share a
memory with me

Light shift—add some house lights.

Does anyone carry a photograph with them?

Do people still do that? Carry photographs in their wallets, in a purse, inside a book?

Not on their cellphones. I hate phones.

Someone offers her a photograph. This section is an open conversation with the audience, sharing photos and memories of loved ones.

You do?

Do you mind showing us the photograph?

Do you mind if I share them with everyone?

Can you tell me a little about this photograph?

Why do you carry them with you?

Thank you so much.

She returns the photographs to their owners.

The Marlboro Man used to tell me the story that he carried a tiny photograph of the two of us—in his wallet, in his chest pocket close to his heart—walking down the streets of Bogotá—holding hands—when I'm a little girl.

It's the rainy season and he's crossing the Magdalena River on his horse. The river is flooded and the current takes him and his horse down the river. When he manages to cross to the other side . . . he reaches for the wallet, but it is gone. And so am I.

EPISODE 8
Julia becomes a prisoner

Shift.

Year three of Julia's calvary.

Julia walks into a stranger's room.

Gets into her bed.

The old woman protests.

Julia hits her on the head.

Next morning they put a lock on Julia's door, from the outside.

Julia becomes a prisoner.

   Beat.

Julia will never sing again.

EPISODE 9
I make the promise

Nat King Cole's "Aquellos ojos verdes" plays. Beatriz places a picture of herself as a child, having soup.

I'm four years old. I'm still living with my grandparents in Medellín.

Julia and Jorge have invited me to their apartment. "For lunch."

Shift—a historical reel plays with a video map on the floor and news images/videos on the wall behind Beatriz.

In this year the Revolutionary Armed Forces of Colombia, the FARC, are established and an armed conflict that will last for more than fifty years begins.

Martin Luther King Jr. receives the Nobel Peace Prize at the age of thirty-five for combating racial inequality through non-violence and civil disobedience.

Glenn Gould stops performing live.

Leonard Cohen publishes *Flowers for Hitler:* "I believe with a perfect faith in all the history I remember, but it's getting harder and harder to remember history."[*]

Quebec passes a law to give wives full legal rights: joint control with her husband over marital property, full control over her own property, and the right to make a contract in her own name. Wow! In Canada women are independent! I told you, revolutions are never quiet.

---

[*]   From "A Migrating Dialogue."

Shift. The video and sound become distorted, conveying the emotional state of the child who is faced with something bigger than herself, and who will eventually throw up out of fear.

Julia and Jorge watch me as I stare at the soup that has been placed in front of me. The soup that will symbolize whether I cross the dividing line between my old life and my new life.

Between my old family and my new family. Where legally I will no longer have a brother and a sister . . .

What they don't know is that I hate soup, like my favourite comic strip character, EVER, Mafalda—a little girl who is preoccupied with world peace, politics, and the state of humanity.

I scan the place. It's a very nice house. Is that my own bedroom? I won't have to share with Vicky and Caliche anymore? But who will play with me? There are no other children in this house . . . Sooo—I will have my own mummy and daddy!

Beatriz takes a deep breath.

I reach for the spoon. I've never seen such a big spoon in my life. I sink the spoon into the soup and lift it to my mouth.

The spoon gets bigger and bigger and my mouth smaller and smaller until I can't contain it anymore. The spoon jumps out of my mouth. Soup bleeds out of every pore in my body. I chase after the spoon. Julia's green eyes rescue me.

JULIA: *(singing)* Sana que sana, colita de rana.

Heal, heal little tail of frog? . . . Is that a lullaby?

JULIA: Si no sanas hoy, sanarás mañana.

If I don't heal today, I will heal tomorrow.

My own personal lullaby!

(realizing) At this exact moment I make the promise to my new mother:

"I will be with you, Julia, by your side, till death do us part"

EPISODE 10
remember, you made a promise

Shift.

Beatriz places a jewellery box.

There are promises we cannot keep. We are human . . . after all.

She opens it and pulls out a ring and a necklace from inside.

Julia outlives Jorge for twenty-six years.

She puts on Julia's ring.

This is a fake wedding ring. Julia is not allowed to keep jewellery in the nursing home. It can be stolen.

I have no idea where she got this ring from.

She holds up Julia's jade necklace.

After Jorge's death, Julia came to visit me in Vancouver.

I bought this for her. The jade matches her eyes.

EPISODE II
how much is Julia hurting?

Shift.

Year four of Julia's calvary.

Julia is trying to escape.

She slips. Falls. Breaks her hip.

I'm in Canada.

I get a call from the nursing home.

I rush back to Medellín.

> BEA: Julia, where does it hurt?
>
> Mommy, how much does it hurt?

EPISODE 12

what kind of a daughter am I?

Video: the stage and performer are lit by an X-ray of a broken hip.

How do you know if someone with Alzheimer's is hurting?

How do you know how much they are hurting?

Julia is released from the hospital.

How do you explain to someone with advanced Alzheimer's—who has just broken their hip—how to get into a taxi?

"Julia, bend your knee, like this, so we can take you home"— HOME?—back to a nursing home!

   Beat.

From now on I will only be able to transport her in an ambulance.

Hospital. Ambulance. Nursing home.

How do you explain to someone with Alzheimer's how to do physiotherapy?

Simple, right?

"Mommy, put your right hand on the bar—Julia, watch me. Julia . . . Julia."

Alzheimer's is not simple.

And then the follow ups, which are a waste of time because Julia can't do physiotherapy—but if I don't take her to the doctor, what kind of a daughter am I?

Nursing home, ambulance, doctor, ambulance, nursing home.

Ambulance, doctor, ambulance, nursing home.

Ambulance, doctor, ambulance, nursing home.

Beat.

Julia's teeth are rotting.

How do you take someone with advanced Alzheimer's to the dentist? You don't.

What kind of a daughter am I?

Beat.

But those are physical pains.

What about the soul?

My mother lives in constant terror. There are no antipsychotic pills that can take her fear away.

I can't take her fear away.

What kind of a daughter am I?

Beat. Shift to the ocean.

Julia was once a lover.

We spend every holiday at the beach house. On the border between Panama and Colombia. The dividing line between two oceans.

Jorge has a ritual: when he arrives at the gate, he takes off his watch.

Jorge and Julia wake up early in the mornings and sneak off for a swim in the ocean, where they make love.

And I . . . am introduced to a way of thinking and the revolutionary songs of Víctor Jara, Mercedes Sosa, Violeta Parra— Anyone here knows these songs?

> *If there are Spanish speakers in the audience, Beatriz asks them to sing one of these songs.*

I know that for most of you these names don't mean much . . . although we Latinx artists insist on writing plays with all these songs and names in them—but for us, we dream of a land of peace, equity, and justice for all.

We dream of individual freedom.

We dream of choices.

We dream of a better quality of life for all.

We dream, we dream, I dream!

(*a confession*) I dream of the day my mother's calvary will end.

> *Beat. Shift.*

Nursing home—

Ambulance—

Doctor—he tells me that most old people, like Julia, die within two years after breaking their hip.

Hope!

Ambulance.

Nursing home.

Beatriz whispers into her mother's ear in Spanish as she places little pieces of paper with the English translation on the table (the text in square brackets).

Mamita déjate ir.   [Let go, Julia.]

¿No quieres ver a papi otra vez?   [Don't you want to see Jorge?]

¿En el cielo?   [In Heaven?]

Pídele a Dios que te lleve.   [Ask God to take you.]

Julia opens her eyes, slaps me on the face, and goes back to sleep.

Beat.

Does she? . . . Want to live like this?

EPISODE 13

what do I believe in?

Beatriz places a glass bowl and crushes pills in it with a spoon while adding water.

Year five of Julia's calvary.

Julia is spoon fed a blend of soft food and antipsychotic pills of different colours and shapes.

Beatriz places a diaper on the table and pours the pill water onto it.

The diapers give her urinary tract infections.

Julia is trying to escape.

She slips. Falls. Breaks her collarbone.

I'm in Canada.

I get a call from the nursing home.

I rush back to Medellín.

Hospital.

Ambulance.

Nursing home.

Ambulance.

Hospital.

Ambulance.

Nursing home.

Ambulance.

Hospital.

Ambulance.

Nursing home.

(*screaming, pleading*) If I believe in you . . . God, are you going to stop Julia's pain, the suffering, the humiliation, her disintegration, her annihilation?

>   *Beat.*

Nothing prepares us. Nothing. Nada.

We never want to imagine a time when we might not be able to walk, talk, or make decisions anymore.

>   *Beat.*

Julia never imagined it.

>   *Beat.*

One day, soon, I will be an old woman.

>   *Beat.*

In the absence of religion, how do I deal with suffering?

Beat.

What do I believe in?

Beat.

Life . . .

EPISODE 14
the cycle of life

Shift. Beatriz is submerged in a video of a thriving underwater environment.

Life begins in water. There has been the same amount of water since prehistoric times. Water never dies. Water is circular. It travels through time, through space, connecting our histories, our thoughts, our memories.

Imagine:

You are a raindrop that falls from a cloud that falls on a patch of soil on the side of a hill.

Many other raindrops join until we burst from the ground and run down the hill.

Down, down, down until we become a river.

Animals drink from us.

Plants feed from us.

Species thrive in us.

Waste flows through us.

When we reach a city, they put walls around us.

When the water is low, they get angry.

When the water is high, they want the dry times again.

EPISODE 15
the end of the line

Shift.

Year six of Julia's calvary.

I am in Canada.

I get a call from a paramedic at the nursing home.

> DOCTOR: Su mamá tiene una infección urinaria. Otra vez.

Urinary tract infection, again.

A long silence.

> DOCTOR: Si yo fuera usted no haría nada y dejaría que la infección se la llevara.

This woman, this anonymous voice at the end of the line, is giving me a window of opportunity: if I don't do anything, the infection will run its course and Julia will die . . . soon.

But without me by her side.

Beatriz takes a deep breath.

No. I made a promise I intend to keep.

Beatriz is submerged in video—her entire body becomes a watershed—a drainage basin with millions of small rivers and streams within her, mapping outwards.

My tears flood the Great Lakes Basin, flowing from Toronto up to Chicago and spilling into the Illinois River, then down through the Mississippi watershed all the way to New Orleans, where they drain into the Gulf of Mexico.

I follow the coastline of Central America along the edge of the Caribbean all the way to Colombia. At Barranquilla I come into the Magdalena River, whose water leads me all the way to Medellín. To my mother.

EPISODE 16

if you were me . . .

Shift—sounds of lament. Julia's voice.

Aaaaaaaaah.

Aaaaaaaaah.

   Ten seconds.

Aaaaaaaaah.

   Ten seconds.

Aaaaaaaaah.

   Ten seconds.

Aaaaaaaaah.

Julia is out of danger. Again.

   Beatriz is asking the audience to put themselves in her place.

Imagine: your mother is out of danger. Again.

You return to the nursing home.

   Shift—brighter, video and lights indicate a nursing home.

A feisty seventy-year-old woman approaches you.

OLD WOMAN: *(to women in the audience)* Usted es la mejor hija del mundo, la mejor, la mejor. Si señora, su mamá es una mamá muy afortunada de tenerla a usted. Muy afortunada. Usted es la mejor hija del mundo. La mejor, la mejor.

Translation: You have been named the Most Devoted Child.

You wheel your mother past the dining room. You still love that story, of when your mother sampled each and every dessert with her spoon.

You pass by the chapel . . .

> *Pause.*

The old bedroom. The lock is still on the outside.

Your mother sleeps by the nursing station now. Her laments disturb the others.

You arrive at the water fountain. And you feel like serenating your mother.

> *Beatriz begins to sing Nat King Cole's "Aquellos ojos verdes."*

Aquellos ojos verdes
De mirada serena
Dejaron en mi alma
Eterna sed de amar

Your mother opens her eyes! She smiles.

> *Beatriz places a photo of Julia smiling, sitting on a wheelchair by the water fountain.*

And this small gesture lets you know that she knows that you are here, with her, by her side.

But the smile does not last long. Your mother's head drops.

She places the photo of Julia with her head dropped.

You'll spend the next month repeating the same path.

Except that your mother will never lift her head again.

Until . . . one day you meet a doctor by the water fountain, next to the bird sanctuary, your mother's favourite place.

He's not just like any doctor.

He is a revolutionary in his own way.

He's here to perform euthanasia on another resident.

Shift. As Beatriz speaks we see the photo of Julia with her head dropped. Text is projected around the photo in square brackets.

As of 2018 euthanasia is legal in the Netherlands, Belgium, Colombia, Luxembourg, Canada, and India.

[Canada 2016: euthanasia becomes legal with Bill C-14. There are no advanced requests for dying.]

[The patient must be conscious and be able to give consent.]

[Not eligible: those suffering from Alzheimer's, Huntington's, Parkinson's, or ALS.]

On November 1 of 2018 Audrey Parker terminates her life before she loses the ability to give consent.

She said, "There is so much negativity and fear around death, but I always believed our first breath gives us life, and it's our final breath that honours our lifetime."

The doctor places a hand on Julia's head. He places a hand on her heart.

> **DOCTOR:** Your mother may last like this for a long time.

> *Beat.*

> Are you afraid of God? You were born in a Catholic country. It's in your DNA.

> *Beat.*

> Let me deal with God, for I know, if he existed, he would not allow Julia to suffer this way.

> *Shift.*

> I begin to smash yet more pills, mix them into her food, spoon-feed her. But the lament doesn't go away. They occur in intervals ten seconds apart. I have timed them perfectly over the last month.

I convene the only two people who can help me: mis hermanitos, my siblings. Vicky and Caliche.

> *Beatriz places the previous drawing of her siblings as children, then a photo of Caliche and Vicky as adults.*

Vicky being Vicky tells it as it is.

> *We hear Vicky's voice speaking Spanish, and Beatriz translates for us.*

VICKY: Tu mamá no necesita más pastillas. Tu mamá lo que necesita es descansar.

Your mother doesn't need more pills: what she needs is to rest.

Silence.

VICKY: Tú no la estás matando.

You're not killing her.

Beat.

VICKY: Lo que estás haciendo es un acto de amor.

What you're doing is an act of love.

VICKY: Un gran acto de amor.

It's a great act of love.

Caliche being Caliche:

We hear Caliche's voice singing "Cachito." Beatriz sings along with him.

Cachito, Cachito, Cachito mío
Pedazo de cielo que Dios me dió
Te miro y te miro y al fin bendigo
Bendigo la suerte de ser tu amor

He says, "Talk to her, you're still her little girl, she will listen."

Beatriz removes photos and places an image of Julia with an oxygen mask, her eyes closed. She continues to fill the space entirely with all the photos from her life that we have seen throughout the play.

All the while, she is singing her mother's song: Nat King Cole's "Aquellos ojos verdes." When she is done the room is filled with images.

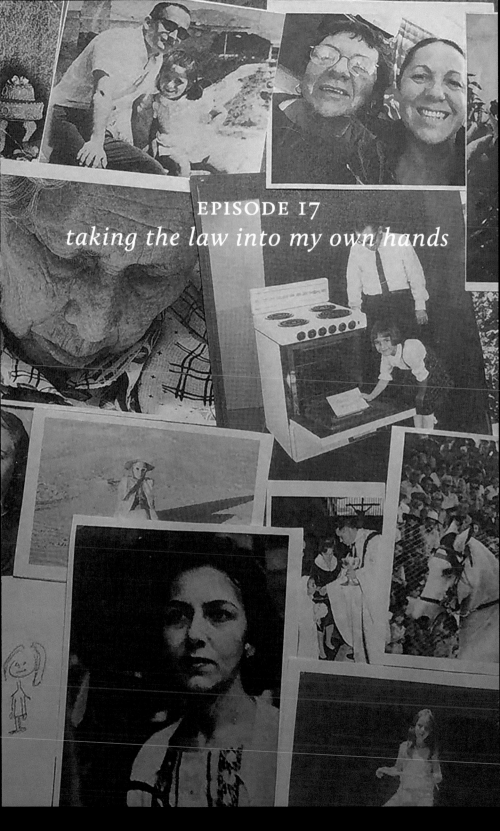

EPISODE 17
taking the law into my own hands

Shift.

Beatriz asks the stage manager for the house lights.

There are some things I cannot say in English, so I'm going to ask if there are some Spanish speakers in the audience who can help me translate.

She finds a volunteer (who speaks from the audience), thanks them, and begins.

Este doctor, llega así no más.	This doctor arrives just like that.
Como llega todo en la vida.	Like everything in life.
Cuando le veo digo:	When I see him I think:
¡Qué hombre más hermoso!	What a beautiful man!
Y luego pienso:	And then I think:
Mi madre saldrá de este mundo en los brazos de un hombre hermoso	My mother will leave this earth in the arms of a beautiful man.
¿Qué más puedo pedirle a la vida?	What more can I ask of life?
Sigo siendo una romántica.	I'm still a romantic.

EPISODE 18
the goodbye

Nat King Cole's "Aquellos ojos verdes" plays in Spanish.

If Julia and I could have had a last supper. This is how I imagine it:

I take her to her favourite restaurant in Medellín. It's really my favourite.

We sit on a beautiful terrace.

She smiles.

She loves being out.

I order for her.

Probably the same thing I order for myself.

Un sanduche de pollo caliente, con champiñones, por favor.

¡Esto es mucho! She says.

No lo es, you can eat it.

All of this ceremony to get to her favourite part of the ritual, dessert.

She savours every bite . . . with her spoon.

EPISODE 19
dying

Shift.

We hear breathing, slowly at first, but intensifying through to the end of this scene.

    BEA: Forgive me for allowing you to suffer for so long—

The doctor stops me.

    DOCTOR: No. This is not about you. Your time to heal will come. This is about your mother. She is crossing now. Julia . . . I want you to imagine that Jorge is in the ocean. Waiting for you. Swim. Swim toward him.

It is time. I have to let go of my mother.

A slow sound and visual shift from the photo collage to the ocean begins. We hear waves.

I close my eyes and see the eternal lovers . . . in the early morning, bathing in the ocean. As they embrace and make love they go under water.

The breathing changes, diminishes. The sound and video slowly fades out.

The dividing line between life and death is just one last breath—

We stay in silence, realizing Julia is gone.

EPISODE 20
the calling

We hear the voices of Ticuna women.

Six years after my mother's death, I'm at an international theatre festival in Bogotá giving a workshop to a group of Ticuna women from the Amazon.

The Ticunas, the Peoples of Land and Water, believe the world is divided into three spaces: the sky above where the creator lives, the middle space—the land we inhabit—and the underwater world where enchanted spirits live in a gigantic house.

I ask the Ticuna women for a lullaby in their language. They don't remember any.

> **BEA:** (*gesturing with her arms*) ¿Una canción que sus mamás les cantaba cuando eran bebes . . . para arrullarlas? ¿Para dormirlas? ¿Para tranquilizarlas?

A Ticuna woman joins me on the stage.

> *Beatriz enacts this.*

> **WOMAN:** Vente pa cá.

She gestures for her teenage daughter to sit on her lap . . .

> *She rocks back and forth as if she has a young woman in her lap. A slow build from her breath to a hopeful sound.*

An ancestral Ticuna lullaby enters the room. The women cry in happiness. "Yes, that's the song our mothers sang to us!"

(fighting for air) I can't breathe!

    ALBA LUCIA: ¡Maestra Beatriz!

La Abuela Alba Lucía, an Elder and a Shaman, approaches me.

    ALBA LUCIA: La memoria está en el cuerpo, maestra Beatriz. Hay que despertarla.

Memory lives in the body. We need to awaken it.

    ALBA LUCIA: Las mamás siempre regresan cuando hay algo que sanar.

Mothers always come back when something needs to be healed.

    ALBA LUCIA: ¿Ha estado en el Amazona maestra Beatriz? Venga a mi casa.

Come to the Amazon, to remember.

EPISODE 21
the healing

The stage begins to change as if Beatriz is travelling—entering the spiritual world. We see footage of the Amazon projected on the wall.

The Amazon is the largest watershed . . . the lungs of the world.

There are over three thousand species of fish and more than two million insect species. Two hundred thousand plants and more than eight hundred mammals, many of which are found nowhere else in the world . . . the pink dolphin!

There are no bridges that cross the Amazon River.

Drums.

I arrive in Puerto Nariño, the land of the Ticunas.

The women gather in Abuela Alba Lucía's home in preparation for the ceremony that will take place over the next two days. A rite of passage that has been prohibited by the Catholic church for over a hundred years. Tonight, we will introduce a toddler to the ancestral languages of dance and body painting.

We walk deep into the jungle. We arrive at La Maloca, the spiritual house—the umbilical cord that connects them to the great white river.

We dance . . . and drum . . . I lose all sense of time. Am I born yet? Am I dead yet? Can I be remembered? Can I be forgotten?

There is a mixture of the lament, Ticuna songs, and "Sana que sana."

Hundreds and hundreds of mothers gather around me.

Beatriz cries.

Ahh . . .

Julia emerges from the underworld and sings:

> **JULIA:** Sana que sana, colita de rana, si no sanas hoy, sanarás mañana.

> **BEA:** Mommy!

We hear a mixture of voices and phrases, including mea culpa. Julia holds a silent heart and offers it to Beatriz. Julia reaches for Beatriz's chest. This is a huge moment of ecstasy, as Julia removes the guilt, replacing it with the new heart. Beatriz takes a deep breath. They both breathe together. One last breath together.

> Pain has no place in my austere kingdom.

Beat.

> It is time.

We hear the drums and go back to the ceremony.

We wet our hands in the juice from the huito fruit and brush the little girls' skin, painting our stories onto her body.

Beatriz's heart begins to beat, loudly.

They say that blood is thicker than water . . .
I say love is thicker than blood.

> *The End*

Beatriz Pizano is a playwright, director, actor, dramaturg, and the founder and artistic director of Aluna Theatre, a company that creates daring, experimental, and political theatre from a TransAmerican perspective. She is a multi-award-winning theatre maker. Her passion for writing was born out of the need to speak about places and peoples that are seldom spoken about, and the desire to bring the heritages, languages, cultures, ancestries, and lands that reside within her onto the stage. She is a fierce artivist who creates spaces and opportunities for racialized artists and who loves to mentor the next generation of daring artists.